The Inner Beauty Series
Defining Your Worth in the Eyes of God

GIVE UP
And
GET FREE

Charisma
HOUSE
Books about Spirit-Led Living

Lisa Bevere

GIVE UP AND GET FREE by Lisa Bevere
Published by Charisma House
A part of Strang Communications Company
600 Rinehart Road
Lake Mary, Florida 32746
www.charismahouse.com

Unless otherwise noted, all Scripture quotations are from the Holy Bible, New International Version. Copyright © 1973, 1978, 1984, International Bible Society. Used by permission.

Scripture quotations marked AMP are from the Amplified Bible. Old Testament copyright © 1965, 1987 by the Zondervan Corporation. The Amplified New Testament copyright © 1954, 1958, 1987 by the Lockman Foundation. Used by permission.

Scripture quotations marked NKJV are from the New King James Version of the Bible. Copyright © 1979, 1980, 1982 by Thomas Nelson, Inc., publishers. Used by permission.

Cover design by Rachel Campbell

Library of Congress Catalog Card Number: 2001099923
International Standard Book Number: 0-88419-843-X

02 03 04 05   87654321
Printed in the United States of America

Contents

Introduction

he inner beauty of a life filled with the glory of God will not be seen when that life still carries the yoke of bondage. In this final booklet in the Inner Beauty Series, you will grasp the importance of losing control to be free—to soar in the glory of God, radiating the inner beauty of a woman of God.

To soar with God, we must learn the difference between a yoke of oppression and God's mantle of anointing. A yoke symbolizes oppression due to heavy responsibility, duty or sin. It represents a burden so great you cannot escape it but are controlled by it. Its bearer has no authority over it; the yoke is the master. It signifies slavery or servitude. The phrase "to break a yoke" means to secure your freedom.

To soar with God, we must learn the difference between a yoke of oppression and God's mantle of anointing.

We are under a yoke of bondage any time we carry what God never intended for us to bear. Often as I minister I can discern when a person is under oppression, depression and fear. Beyond the recognition of their outward effects, I can also sense the yoke's weight and strain on their shoulders. In the spirit I can see the person bent under a weight that is too heavy for him or her to carry. The person struggles and labors against it, but the yoke always oppresses him or her in the end. The yoke is not the person's to carry.

On the other hand, a mantle represents protection, warmth, covering and position. It was designed to be totally nonrestrictive, a sleeveless cloak worn over other garments. It was large enough to carry and conceal things within its folds. At night it was used as a bed covering.

A mantle's detail and ornamentation represented social standing or position. Samuel's mantle was fashioned by his mother as a miniature of the priestly garment. Joseph's mantle incorporated many colors, calling attention to him and exalting him above his brothers. Isaiah and John the Baptist wore mantles of animal skin, signifying their unique and similar prophetic callings.

A mantle covers our nakedness, conceals our faults, carries supplies and announces our authority or position to those around us. When we are in proper submission to Christ, we are covered and cloaked in all that His mantle represents.

This principle applies to everyone—woman or man, married or single. Christ is your priest, protection and provision. Dare to trust Him and the authority structure He has established. He is our Husband and Advocate with the Father.

BRINGING IT HOME

Let us not confine this principle to male/female relationships. This applies to any area where we are faced with a decision to hang on to the old or go on to the new. It's about leaving the comfortable and moving to the unexpected.

Ask God to show you the difference between a yoke and a mantle.

Think about the past year of your life. Would you say, as I did, that you have been stressed out? Are you burning yourself to the ground trying to stay in control of areas that God never meant for you to shoulder? Are you in control—and hating it?

Ask God to show you the difference between a yoke and a mantle. Remember that a yoke enslaves you by making you responsible for something that is not your responsibility and not under your control. A mantle, on the other hand, rests on you when you operate in the authority and anointing that God has ordained for you.

Any responsibility you take up that God did not ordain for you will put you in a yoke. However, when God gives you a calling to fulfill, His mantle of anointing will help you to accomplish it. If you stay bound to your yoke of oppression, you will not be able to soar as a woman of God. Read on to discover for yourself how to lose control and relinquish your yoke. That's the only way to reveal the inner beauty of the woman God wants you to be.

Adapted from Lisa Bevere, *Out of Control and Loving It!*, 94–96, 101–102.

INNER BEAUTY TIP

JESUS WANTED THE
WORD OF GOD MORE THAN
NECESSARY BREAD.
HE DENIED HIMSELF THE
IMMEDIATE AND WAITED UPON
THE ETERNAL.

God's Secrets

The secret of the LORD is with those who fear Him, and He will show them His covenant.

—PSALM 25:14, NKJV

God shares insights and secrets with those who fear Him. The Book of Psalms talks about God's secrets. The Bible tells us the story of a widow woman named Anna, who was very old. She holds a very important historical significance:

She never left the temple but worshiped night and day, fasting and praying. Coming up to them [Joseph, Mary and baby Jesus] at that very moment, she gave thanks to God and spoke about the child to all who

were looking forward to the redemption of
Jerusalem.

—Luke 2:37–38

This very old woman who prayed and fasted
could see better than the priest and the young people around her. She recognized Jesus as the long-
awaited Messiah when He was only eight days old.
The Pharisees couldn't even recognize Him at
thirty-three, when He was casting out devils. Yet
this elderly mother of the faith knew Him as He
lay cradled in His mother's arms.

She was a true prophetess who encouraged
those who were watching and waiting for Israel's
redemption. Her prayers and fasting gave her
prophetic insight.

Once you have relinquished control to the Lord
and have learned to live free and unencumbered
by the bondages of your past, you are ready to
grow into the woman of God you were meant to
be. One of the Christian disciplines that can help
you do that is fasting. In this chapter we will take
a closer look as how fasting can help you reveal
your inner beauty.

You may or may not be a position to fast food.

2

But everyone is in a position to fast something. It may be TV, telephone, magazines, sports, shopping or hobbies. All of us have areas in which we hide ourselves or waste time.

Every believer should fast periodically.

I challenge you to go before our Father and ask Him, by the power of the Holy Spirit, to expose any areas that could be fasted.

Every believer should fast periodically. It is an act of separation to our Father. Some of you may be anorexic or bulimic. You need to fast all the images that have driven you to such abuse. Jesus gave us invaluable insight on fasting:

> Moreover, when you fast, do not be like the hypocrites, with a sad countenance. For they disfigure their faces that they may appear to men to be fasting. Assuredly, I say to you, they have their reward.
>
> —MATTHEW 6:16, NKJV

The one who fasts must do so with the right motivation. Jesus often berated the Pharisees for their religious, pious fastings done only for the attention it brought to them. Matthew 6:16 advises us to not be like the hypocrites.

Hypocrite is another name for impostor. An *impostor* is one who deceives others by the assumed character or false pretenses. The Pharisees pretended to fast unto the Lord when it was really done for the accolades of man. Their focus was on their pious religious appearance, and their reward was the awe of man. They wanted to be great among men. But they received nothing from God's hand. You must choose between the reward of man and the reward of God. The religious fast is rewarded by man, while the broken and contrite are rewarded by God. Jesus continued:

> But you, when you fast, anoint your head and wash your face, so that you do not appear to men to be fasting, but to your Father who is in the secret place; and your Father who sees in secret will reward you openly.
>
> —MATTHEW 6:17–18, NKJV

If we are not hungry for God, it is because we have allowed our souls to be satisfied or satiated with other things. One morning when I was praying, I sensed the need for more of a hunger for God. I asked God to impart this hunger in me. At the time, I was recording my prayers in my journal; I waited for a response from God.

> If we are not hungry for God, it is because we have allowed our souls to be satisfied or satiated with other things.

As fast as I could write, He answered me. He showed me I was the one responsible for my hunger level. He told me that if I wasn't hungry, it was because I was already full. Filled with the cares of this world. Filled with the pleasures and distractions of this world. He said that if I wanted to hunger in the midst of the abundance of things, I would need to fast. Fast the things that would distract, comfort or distress me.

I was nursing my fourth son at the time, and I knew God was not calling me to fast food. He was calling me to fast other things that pulled me from His presence. I fasted TV, magazines, telephone calls that were not business related and desserts. I rearranged my schedule to accommodate prayer and Bible reading.

I did this for about a month, and when the month was over, I had lost my appetite for many of the things I'd laid aside. I sensed an increased discernment. I had previously been desensitized by the abundance of noise, voices and distractions. Now it was easier to hear God's voice.

The natural noise level in my house (with four young boys) had not varied; it was the static and noise in my mind that quieted. You may even now be saying, "Sounds great, but who has the time?" If we reserve fasting only for the times when we can physically leave or lock ourselves away, we will not fast.

As a mother, I am in a season where my children have legitimate demands on my time. God didn't tell me to check into a hotel room. He probably knew I would pass out and sleep the whole time. He wanted me to develop the ability to fast within my home and lifestyle.

God wants to be an integral part of our life every day, not just when we are on the mountain spiritually. I have had to develop a listening ear, one that can hear amid the din and noise of a full household. I have learned to listen while I take a shower, do dishes and sort laundry.

This may shock you, but most of the time on my knees has been spent emptying my heart and repenting. Once this is done, I can usually hear God's voice whenever He desires to speak to me. When I prepare for a service, I study and make pages of notes. Often I never use them. I do the notes for my sake—to put my mind at ease. The real preparation for the service comes when I confess and cleanse my heart before the Lord.

This time of cleansing allows the Holy Spirit to flow through me. It separates the precious and holy (God's Word and anointing) from the vile (my agenda or prejudice). I separate myself for whatever time it takes until I sense this separation has taken place.

Fasting brings many benefits into our lives. Here are a few of them:

1. FASTING CREATES A NEW HUNGER.

> So we fasted and petitioned our God about this, and he answered our prayer.
>
> —EZRA 8:23

When you fast...you become hungry. At first it may be hunger for food or whatever you are fasting, but as the initial hunger pangs or longings cease, a new desire or hunger is formed. Fasting causes you to hunger in the midst of abundance.

2. FASTING INCREASES SENSITIVITY TO GOD.

> There was also a prophetess, Anna...She never left the temple but worshiped night and day, fasting and praying. Coming up to them at that very moment, she gave thanks to God and spoke about the child to all who were looking forward to the redemption of Jerusalem.
>
> —LUKE 2:36–38

From this account of the widow Anna, we can see that fasting and prayer had developed such a keen sensitivity in her that she perceived the Christ child at a few days old. She could hear clearly what God was saying.

I have found myself more sensitive after a period of fasting. Our family decided to fast television for a month. During this time we spent time together playing, talking and praying. It put us in closer touch with each other, and consequently John and I became more sensitive toward our children's needs, fears and hopes. When the television was turned back on, the difference was evident. What disturbed me before now grieved me. Each of us viewed violence as a personal violation. Our insight had been honed when the constant barrage of conflicting images was removed. Previously, we had not been watching anything so horrible—it was just that the normal became so violating after a time of separation.

3. FASTING WORKS HUMILITY.

> Yet when they were ill, I put on sackcloth and humbled myself with fasting. When

my prayers returned to me unanswered…

—PSALM 35:13

When we fast, we deny ourselves that which might satisfy us. When we deny ourselves food, we often feel our natural strength waning. In our weakness we find ourselves more dependent. It is a confrontation with the flesh, a time when we deny it satisfaction and provision. It is a time of turning aside from what we can provide and turning toward what God alone can give. This is often the setting for a confrontation between the spirit and the flesh. I personally find out just how strong a hold my flesh has on me when I fast. This revelation alone is humbling, but in order for the fast to be successful you must allow it to work humility in you. This replaces and reorders your perspective.

Fasting is a confrontation
with the flesh, a time when
we deny it satisfaction
and provision.

After forty days in the wilderness, Jesus was hungry physically. Satan came to tempt Him to use His position as the Son of God to create bread from stone. But instead Jesus humbled Himself and answered:

> It is written: "Man does not live on bread alone, but on every word that comes from the mouth of God."
>
> —MATTHEW 4:4

He wanted the Word of God more than necessary bread. He chose living bread over baked bread, and He became the Bread of Life. He denied Himself the immediate and waited upon the eternal.

4. FASTING CHASTENS OR DISCIPLINES.

> When I wept and chastened my soul with fasting, that became my reproach.
>
> —PSALM 69:10, NKJV

We have already discussed this benefit, but let's look at it from another angle. When my children are disobedient or irresponsible with a toy, person or privilege, we remove it until it is once again in the proper perspective. In some instances, grounding could be viewed as a fast—a fast of privileges, friends or sports. After they are returned, there is a new appreciation.

5. FASTING CHANGES OUR APPETITE.

> While they were worshiping the Lord and fasting, the Holy Spirit said, "Set apart for me Barnabas and Saul for the work to which I have called them."
>
> —ACTS 13:2

If you've developed an appetite for something, you can crave it as long as you are eating it. For example, I am a fan of dark chocolate. Only dark chocolate appeals to me. If you were to offer me milk chocolate, I would not even want it. At a certain time each month I feel a sudden and strong urge for this pure dark chocolate. I crave it; when I have had it, I am fine for another month.

One time I was given a large supply of dark chocolate; I could have a piece each day if I wanted it. It wasn't long before I found myself *needing* my daily piece. Soon my supply was exhausted. For a few days I found myself returning to the pantry, hoping to find just one more piece somewhere. If

I found a piece, then the cravings were gone. I had become accustomed to daily chocolate. When I was forced by lack of supply to fast from it, then I no longer hungered for it.

A fast is a break in our daily routine. It overcomes past cravings and restores or renews a fresh and new appetite. Whenever I come off a fast, I am hungry for healthy food. I am hungry for something new and fresh in my personal life as well. I want to leave behind the old and embrace the new.

6. FASTING INCREASES OUR CAPACITY.

> Go, gather together all the Jews who are in Susa, and fast for me. Do not eat or drink for three days, night or day. I and my maids will fast as you do. When this is done, I will go to the king, even though it is against the law. And if I perish, I perish.
>
> —ESTHER 4:16

This fast prepared Esther to overcome the fear of man and, even greater, her fear of death. This fast increased her capacity for self-sacrifice while it imparted wisdom. The survival of a nation depended on her willingness to lay down her life.

She knew it was more than she could face in her present condition with her present information, so she drew on God's strength.

As I thought about Esther's response to God, and the supernatural strength she received from Him, God told me, "If you want more than what you've seen, you'll need to be more than you've been." Fasting positions you for just such an increase.

7. FASTING BRINGS ANSWERS TO PRAYER.

> Then you will call, and the LORD will answer; you will cry for help, and he will say: Here am I. If you do away with the yoke of oppression, with the pointing finger and malicious talk…
>
> —ISAIAH 58:9

A godly fast will bring answered prayer. It is the atmosphere for answers to questions, direction, help and the revelation of God. It is a time when He says, "Here I am…I'm over here. Come to Me." This revelation may come through His Word or as a still, small voice or by a strong confirmation of what He has previously shown us.

14

8. FASTING LEADS TO QUICK HEALING.

> Then your light will break forth like the dawn, and your healing will quickly appear.
> —ISAIAH 58:8

God set up the fast as a manner of healing His people, a time when the darkness of oppression, depression or infirmity is dispelled by light such as the dawn. When this light breaks forth, then healing soon follows. This could mean many things. It could be a revelation of sin, which, when repented of, allows healing to spring forth. It could mean a revelation of His will or Word that brings healing and freedom where there had been darkness or ignorance. This healing could be physical, mental or spiritual.

Even natural medicine supports this. Many illnesses occur in the digestive system. A short fast gives your body a chance to refocus its energies on *healing* instead of on eating. (Please contact a physician before undertaking a fast if you are ill.)

9. Fasting opens the door to God's protection and provision.

> Then your righteousness will go before you, and the glory of the LORD will be your rear guard.
>
> —Isaiah 58:8

God promised to be a guard before us and after us. A fast renews your righteousness and sends it on before you. Then as you give God the glory, He returns righteousness as your rear guard.

10. Fasting looses chains of injustice.

> Is not this the kind of fasting I have chosen: to loose the chains of injustice and untie the cords of the yoke…
>
> —Isaiah 58:6

The kind of fast into which God leads us has the power to loose any unjust chains that bind us. It also unties the cords tethering us to any yoke. But this application is not limited merely to a personal liberation for us—it represents God's desire to see us reach out and untie the ties that bind others and remove the chains of oppression.

11. FASTING FREES THE OPPRESSED AND BREAKS EVERY YOKE.

> Is not this the kind of fasting I have chosen...to set the oppressed free and break every yoke?
>
> —ISAIAH 58:6

A fast is a time when we take our eyes off ourselves and our needs and look around at the oppression and pain of others. In response we learn to reach out in compassion and help, becoming agents of healing.

Jesus said that His burden was easy and His yoke was light. When we are carrying a burden other than His, it is cumbersome, awkward and heavy. There is nothing more frustrating than feeling responsible for something over which you have no authority. It will weigh you down with hopelessness and frustration.

During a fast, God checks these areas in our lives and exposes the yokes of fear, worry, stress and turmoil. He removes them and readjusts His yoke for our life, the one that keeps us dependent upon Him. If you are feeling weighed down, perhaps you are carrying too much.

12. FASTING MOTIVATES US TO PROVIDE FOOD FOR THE NEEDY.

Is it not to share your food with the hungry…
—ISAIAH 58:7

The benefit is kind of obvious—if you are not eating because of a fast, then you are free to share your portion with those less fortunate. Maybe you should give away any food lingering in your refrigerator or pantry that has a significant pull on you. (I personally am never tempted by a can of beans, but chocolate is another story!) Share with someone else, but don't proclaim or herald your fast… just give to them. I used to find it very hard to keep my fasting a secret because I felt I had to give a reason or justification for everything I did. It is all right to just say, "No, thank you, not today; I have other plans," to a lunch or dinner invitation. We do not need to explain further.

Inward transformation positions us for the promotion of the Lord.

Fasting is not a burden but a privilege. It is intimate and private. It originated in the secret place between you and God. He waits in the secret place for you to join Him. After we visit with Him in secret, He will reward us openly. Inward transformation brings about outward anointing, blessing and provision. Inward transformation positions us for the promotion of the Lord.

Even in the midst of opposition, the believer who fasts as an act of separation from the world and unto God receives the rewards of God. You'll be amazed at how this discipline can help to reveal your inner beauty.

Adapted from Lisa Bevere, *You Are Not What You Weigh*, 119–131.

INNER BEAUTY TIP

WE ARE LOOKING

FOR SOMETHING

WE HAVE NEVER SEEN,

YET WE WILL RECOGNIZE IT

WHEN WE SEE IT.

2

"I Have Found It"

A cord of three strands is not quickly broken.
—Ecclesiastes 4:12

n the previous booklets in the Inner Beauty Series we have talked a lot about what hinders our inner beauty from shining forth. In these final chapters we will concentrate on what it is that allows our beauty to be seen.

Perhaps you have felt like exclaiming, "What inner beauty? I can't seem to find anything beautiful in my life!" Maybe you even feel that due to the circumstances of your life, you have lost the ability to shine and radiate for God.

Whenever we have lost an item, we will search in

one place, then another. At first it might be discouraging when we don't find the misplaced item where we initially search. But each disappointment only narrows the options. We may say, "I've looked in the closet, my dresser, my purses, my coat pockets, and I still can't find it! It must be somewhere I have not thought to look." Then we quiet ourselves and for the first time stop our frantic and sometimes panicked search. We sit or kneel down and say, "God, I can't find what I am looking for. Holy Spirit, please quicken to my memory where it is."

"GOD TALKED TO ME!"

My second son, Austin, was four years old when we bought him some Legos that were all his own. Before this, most of his toys were his older brother's first, and he shared them. Or if he did receive Legos of his own, his older brother would quickly negotiate with him and talk him into combining them into one collection. On his birthday, we bought Austin a little Lego motorcycle police set that was his alone.

We sat him down and explained, "These are just for you. They aren't for Addison, and they are too grown up for Alexander. They're yours!"

Austin beamed as he carried the new Lego set off to a place of honor in the toy room. Whenever anyone else tried to take the Legos, we'd remind, "Those are Austin's. You may only play with them if he has given you permission."

A month or so went by without any incident or loss. Then it happened. I was in the shower one morning when a frantic knock sounded at my door. Austin appeared, his face red and streaked with tears.

"Mom, I can't find my Lego guy!"

Austin's "Lego guy" was a policeman about two inches high that rode a plastic motorcycle. My oldest son was at school, and Alexander was down for a nap. I could see that Austin was panicked, but I needed to finish my shower, so I made a suggestion.

"Go look on the dresser by your bed."

> "God, help Austin find his Lego guy. It means so much to him."

Austin's blond curls bounced as he whirled around and out the bathroom door. I could see that he was on a mission. I continued to wash my hair and prayed under my breath, "God, help Austin find his Lego guy. It means so much to him."

God immediately gave me an answer, though I had not expected one. (Yes, a lot of times this happens to me in the shower.)

"Tell him to kneel down and ask Me, and I will show him where it is."

Moments later, Austin again burst into my bathroom.

"Mom, it's not there!" His little face reflected his desperation.

I thought for a moment, trying to suggest a more unusual place to find the toy.

"See if it fell into the silk tree under the loft. A lot of toys fall in. Shake its branches; I bet it's there," I confidently offered.

Immediately I sensed God's displeasure. I reasoned, *But God, Austin is a four-year-old! If I tell him You are going to talk to him and You don't, it will devastate him! He won't understand it.*

I could tell God wasn't convinced. So I bartered,

If he comes in again and hasn't found it, I'll tell him what You said.

Secretly I began to rush my shower in the hope of getting out before Austin came in again. Then I could help him look. As I was drying off, the door flew open again. Austin was very discouraged and crying.

"It's lost, Mommy! I can't find it. Please come help me!"

I looked at his sweet, innocent, trusting face. He was confident that if only I helped him, he would find his Lego guy. I could be the hero—or I could repeat the Holy Spirit's words to me.

> ## "Tell him to kneel down and ask Me, and I will show him where it is."

I lowered my voice to calm him. "Austin, while I was in the shower God told me that if you will go upstairs, kneel down and ask Him where your Lego guy is, He will show you."

He calmed down and with a serious face turned and left for the loft. My heart flew into a panic: *What if He didn't? What if I hadn't heard from God and only imagined that I had? I'll have a bigger mess than a lost Lego man!* I began to pray again when the Holy Spirit questioned me, "Whose child is this?"

I was always saying that my children were not my own but God's; now this was where the rubber met the road.

"He's Yours," I answered.

A few moments later I heard jumping and shouting overhead, followed by rapid and heavy footsteps down the stairs. In a moment Austin was in my room, and clutched in his fist was his little Lego man! He was jumping up and down with joy and yelling, "God talked to me! God talked to me!"

Austin was oblivious to finding the lost toy, because he had heard from his Maker! We both hugged and jumped until he settled down. Wrapped in my towel, I knelt and asked, "Austin, tell me what happened."

"I went upstairs, knelt down and asked God— and He told me my Lego guy was on top of the bookcase," Austin answered matter-of-factly. He seemed surprised that I would question him since he had merely followed my instructions.

Retrieval of a Lego guy from the top of the bookcase would involve my four-year-old son's climbing up and standing on the arm of the sofa. The toy could only have arrived on top of the bookcase if thrown there by a brother or placed there by an adult. It was impossible for Austin to reach that height without climbing.

"God talked to me! God talked to me!"

"How did you hear God? What did He say?" I probed.

He cocked his head and replied, "He talked to me in my head and said, 'It is on the bookshelf.'" Then the whole concept of God talking to him over-whelmed him again, and Austin began hopping and chanting, "God talked to me! God talked to me!"

Whenever he looks for something and cannot

find it, I always remind him of this incident, and Austin will go off to pray. It is usually just a matter of time before the lost item is retrieved. It is yet another chance for my son to acknowledge God's guidance in his life.

A THREEFOLD CORD

We are not looking for a mere object but for a blending of truth. We are looking for something we have never seen, yet we will recognize it when we see it. I believe the true measure of a woman is a threefold cord.

> A cord of three strands is not quickly broken.
> —ECCLESIASTES 4:12

This cord reveals the beauty of a woman of God.

This triune cord represents an intricate and intertwined balance in the value or measure of an individual. This cord reveals the beauty of a woman of God. The number *three* is repeated frequently throughout the Bible as a divine representation of balance. The first thread in our cord is *our faith in God*. Before we go on to the second thread, I would like for us to pray and again acknowledge God's hand in our helping us reveal our inner beauty:

> *Father, please show me my own inner beauty. I've looked in many places and have not found Your beauty there. The past was filled with pain and joys that obscured the beauty You had placed within me. The possessions that surround me are lifeless and cannot radiate Your beauty. My friends and family are searching for the beauty You have placed within them. My profession, marital status or looks are what I do or whom I relate to or what I look like; they hinder Your beauty within from shining forth.*
>
> *I hold a strand of faith, and I believe that You are, and that You will reward my diligent search for truth. As I go further, give me eyes to see, ears to hear and a heart to perceive and understand. Amen.*

When I began to write this series, I was searching

for the inner beauty within my own life. I was uncertain and hesitant about how to reflect the beauty of God's love within my life.

God assured me that if I would write, He would show me. I agreed and trusted God for His answers. He began by expanding my list of what that beauty was not. Below is a brief list. Though it is not exhaustive, these were the things that most pertained to me. Some are obvious; others are not.

Your inner beauty is not—

- *What you do*—wife, mother, career
- *Who you know*—friends, associations
- *What you know*—education and intelligence
- *What you've done*—accomplishments, your past
- *What you wear*—hair, clothing, image, makeup
- *What you weigh*—body size and shape
- *What you own (have)*—possessions, home, cars

- *Where you've been*—travel and experience
- *Your marital status*—married, single, widowed, divorced
- *The color of your skin*—racial, cultural, ethnic
- *Your gender*—male or female

The true gospel is always simple and pure. It transcends culture, gender, income, age and time. It is truth for everyone, the truth for whosoever will. It was true yesterday. It is true today. It will be true tomorrow. Only truths in this category can set you free, for others vary with age, health, income, lifestyle and relationships.

God anchors His measure of truth to an eternal scale and strikes a threefold balance.

God would never attach the true worth of an individual to anything so frivolous. He is altogether wise and perfect, so He anchors His measure of truth to an eternal scale and strikes a threefold balance. The second chord we will discuss in this chapter; the third, in the next. Please read the following verses as though you had never read them before:

> If I speak in the tongues of men and of angels, but have not love, I am only a resounding gong or a clanging cymbal. If I have the gift of prophecy and can fathom all mysteries and all knowledge, and if I have a faith that can move mountains, but have not love, I am nothing. If I give all I possess to the poor and surrender my body to the flames, but have not love, I gain nothing.
>
> Love is patient, love is kind. It does not envy, it does not boast, it is not proud. It is not rude, it is not self-seeking, it is not easily angered, it keeps no record of wrongs. Love does not delight in evil but rejoices with the truth. It always protects, always trusts, always hopes, always perseveres.
>
> Love never fails. But where there are prophecies, they will cease; where there are tongues, they will be stilled; where there is knowledge, it will pass away. For we know

in part and we prophesy in part, but when perfection comes, the imperfect disappears. When I was a child, I talked like a child, I thought like a child, I reasoned like a child. When I became a man, I put childish ways behind me. Now we see but a poor reflection as in a mirror; then we shall see face to face. Now I know in part; then I shall know fully, even as I am fully known.

And now these three remain: faith, hope and love. But the greatest of these is love.

—1 Corinthians 13:1–13

The Second Strand

The second measure of a woman's inner beauty is *her love for God*. Scan the above scripture text again, and notice there is no mention of the love between a man and a woman—nor of parents for their children. These are not mentioned, because the love represented in this scripture supersedes the natural love of family. *We are not measured by how we are loved by others but by how much we love.*

The love described here is God's love shed abroad in our hearts. It is the love that encourages us to look closer into that dim and poor reflection and fall in love with Christ in us, the hope of glory.

We are not measured by how we are loved by others but by how much we love.

Our reflection is clouded and distorted by our own visage, but the day will come when we will stand *face to face* and *know fully* as we are *fully known*. Our love for God will exceed our love of man and our love of self.

Paul begins by describing spiritual gifts and miraculous feats of faith. Then he describes great personal sacrifice to the point of death. He surmises that without love, all of these are as nothing. They have no value. Gifts, knowledge, faith, works and sacrifice are all worthless without love.

Paul then describes the attributes and characteristics of love. The list of patience, kindness, humility, selflessness and tolerance seems pale in comparison with the incredible feats described above. Then, by the Spirit, he makes this proclamation: *Love never fails.*

All else passes away, but love endures. Love is eternal. God's love for us never perishes, never varies, never falters, never ceases. Because it is never-ending, it is incorruptible. The capacity for this love is in each of us, for we are commanded to:

> "Love the Lord your God with all your heart and with all your soul and with all your mind." This is the first and greatest commandment. And the second is like it: "Love your neighbor as yourself." All the Law and the Prophets hang on these two commandments.
>
> —MATTHEW 22:37–40

God does not require us to do things that are possible. He requires us to do things that are *impossible* apart from Him. His commandments are only two and are listed in order of their pre-eminence. First, we are to love God with *all* our heart, soul, mind and strength. After we have spent ourselves entirely in this pursuit, then we will be empowered to love our neighbor as ourselves.

Self-love is always a work of the flesh and an exercise in frustration and futility.

For so long we have had it backward. We have tried to love ourselves so we could love our neighbors. We have tried to love our neighbors when we didn't love ourselves. But God is calling us to love Him so we can love our neighbors and ourselves.

If we spend ourselves on loving ourselves, we will become the focus. *Self-love* is always a work of the flesh and an exercise in frustration and futility. We will always find fault in ourselves. We will find iniquity, disappointment and imperfection in ourselves. We can study our past and study ourselves and still not find any true answers.

If we spend ourselves trying to love others, they will become our focus. We will soon see their flaws and imperfections. People will fail and disappoint us. They will break their promises and reject and betray us. Even if all relationships remain perfect, we can love our husbands and our children and still not love God.

God wants us to love Him.

> Knowledge puffs up, but love builds up. The man who thinks he knows something does not yet know as he ought to know. But the man who loves God is known by God.
> —1 Corinthians 8:1–3

Let's pull that phrase out and say it so you will hear it:

> The woman who loves God is known by God.

It is of utmost importance that God knows us. Without this recognition, we cannot enter into His kingdom or reflect His glory. There are a lot of references in the New Testament where individuals are told, "Depart! I don't know you." They thought they knew *Him*, but He did not know *them*. By loving God, we are transformed into the image of His Son and therefore recognized as His children. Every father can recognize his own children. He sees in their form and features the shadow of his own. God knows we can't even love Him without

37

His help, so He has supplied a selfless love for us:

> Dear friends, let us love one another, for love comes from God. Everyone who loves has been born of God and knows God.
>
> —1 JOHN 4:7

By loving God, we are transformed into the image of His Son and therefore recognized as His children.

Love comes from God, not from feelings, relationships or from our circumstances. It is a divine impartation from our Father.

> We love because he first loved us.
>
> —1 JOHN 4:19

We can love Him because it is safe to do so. We will not be rejected. His love will not cease or change. It is limitless. When we look deep into the glass, we see an ever-increasing revelation of that love. The love of God frees us from fear.

> There is no fear in love. But perfect love drives out fear, because fear has to do with punishment. The one who fears is not made perfect in love.
>
> —1 John 4:18

If you are afraid, it is because you are trying to love others without first experiencing a love for God. You will always fail and fall short if you first attempt the love of others when you have not wholeheartedly pursued the love of God. In the love of God, you will find His gracious forgiveness so you can, in turn, forgive graciously. You find His love, and therefore you can love.

Remember when you first got saved? You loved God so much because He had forgiven you of so much. It was easy to love others without even trying because you were so overwhelmed by the love of God.

We have no less need of His mercy now than we did then. In fact, we should love Him more because we know Him more.

Now is the time to return our love to Him.

But often we get our eyes off God and back onto ourselves or onto our brothers and sisters. Our vision becomes dim, and our love waxes cold. We focus on our failures at loving instead of on the source of love. Now is the time to return our love to Him. We've made the mistake of trying to love others to prove our love for Him. We need to ask Him to renew our love for Him. We need to ask Him:

> Place me like a seal over your heart, like a seal on your arm; for love is as strong as death…It burns like blazing fire, like a mighty flame.
>
> —Song of Solomon 8:6

We have been like wayward wives who loved others and forgot our first true love. We lavished our works, affections and strength on the "husband" of religion and forgot the love of our youth. Some no longer sense His love, but He has promised:

"In a surge of anger I hid my face from you for a moment, but with everlasting kindness I will have compassion on you," says the Lord your Redeemer.

—Isaiah 54:8

The first true measure of a woman's beauty is her faith in God. The second is her love for God. His love is everlasting, regardless of our faithlessness. It is one standard by which He measures us.

> # The first true measure of a woman's beauty is her faith in God. The second is her love for God.

Adapted from Lisa Bevere, *The True Measure of a Woman*, 145–156.

INNER BEAUTY TIP

THE NOBLE WOMAN HAS LEARNED
THE SECRET OF A BEAUTY THAT
RADIATES FROM WITHIN.
HER INWARD PURITY WORKS
AN OUTWARD RADIANCE.
SHE ALLOWS HER MEASURE OF FAITH
TO DEVELOP BOTH THE LOVE OF GOD
AND THE FEAR OF THE LORD
IN HER LIFE.

3

The Third Strand

Charm is deceptive, and beauty is fleeting; but a woman who fears the LORD is to be praised.

—PROVERBS 31:30

he third strand of a woman's inner beauty is reverent and worshipful *fear of the Lord.* In the last chapter, we discussed how God recognizes us by the imparted love we have for Him. In this chapter, we will examine the importance of holy fear. This essential ingredient is put into perspective in Proverbs 31:29–31:

"Many women do noble things, but you surpass them all." Charm is deceptive, and beauty is fleeting; but a woman who fears the LORD is to be praised. Give her the

reward she has earned, and let her works
bring her praise at the city gate.

The woman who fears the
Lord will be praised.

Again, this measure is available to "whosoever
will." It is another one of God's measures that is
equally accessible to everyone. It is not dependent
on intelligence, talent, looks, ability or age. It is not
a function of learning, experience, knowledge,
wealth, poverty, social status, profession, possessions, marital status, children, associations, loca-
tion, size, height, weight or skin or hair color. It
surpasses our past failures and successes. It out-
ranks any position of leadership and overpowers
any anointing on our lives.

The woman who fears the Lord will be praised.
Her reverent fear will earn her an eternal reward.
Her works will bring her praise at the gate.

The fear of the Lord is the final thread that
intertwines and knots all the other strands

together. Before we dig deeper into what the fear of the Lord is, let's look closer at our example.

THE "PROVERBS WOMAN"

Just who was this virtuous woman described in Proverbs 31? Most scholars agree that she is Bathsheba. I believe God purposely chose Bathsheba for a number of reasons. First, she was a woman with a past.

Bathsheba was summoned by King David after he had watched her bathe. It was never her intent to seduce David. He spied her from high on his roof as she was completing her purification rite after her menstrual cycle.

> One evening David got up from his bed and walked around on the roof of the palace. From the roof he saw a woman bathing. The woman was very beautiful... (She had purified herself from her uncleanness.)
>
> —2 SAMUEL 11:2, 4

It is hard for us to imagine life in the culture of biblical times. Messengers arrived at Bathsheba's door and escorted her to the king. When someone was summoned by the king, there was no such thing as disobedience. David slept with Bathsheba, then sent her away. Alone, she felt the weight and guilt of her adultery. Weeks later, she awoke sick and tired and realized she was with child. Alone and afraid, she sent word of her pregnancy to the king.

David responded by trying to manipulate her husband, Uriah, into sleeping with Bathsheba to cover his guilt and to make Uriah think he had been the one to get his wife pregnant. But Uriah was loyal to the king and would not allow himself the pleasure of enjoying his wife and home when everyone else in David's army was in the thick of battle. So David arranged for Uriah's death.

Bathsheba was a woman who had known pain. Forget Hollywood's interpretation of the story. Second Samuel 11:26 clearly says, "When Uriah's wife heard that her husband was dead, she mourned for him." There is no record of Abigail mourning the death of her husband. Abigail was excited to be free and came immediately to David. But look closely at the description of Bathsheba's marriage to David:

46

> After the time of mourning was over, David had her brought to his house, and she became his wife and bore him a son.
>
> —2 Samuel 11:27

Bathsheba had endured many things. There is almost no record of her feelings in the matter. She became David's wife and bore him a child. But notice with whom God was upset:

> But the thing David had done displeased the Lord.
>
> —2 Samuel 11:27

There was no mention of Bathsheba's share in the guilt. Less than a year after the death of her first husband, Bathsheba's firstborn son was struck ill and died by the hand of the Lord (2 Sam. 12:15). Imagine what life was like for her.

Bathsheba shared David with his other wives, ones who would certainly be jealous. As she walked the private corridors of the palace, I'm sure she was the object of gossip and scorn. Then her sole comfort—her precious child—was killed because of the sin of David.

With the death of this child, David went to

comfort Bathsheba, and she became pregnant with Solomon. From Solomon's birth forward, the Lord loved this child and confirmed His love and acceptance of this tiny life through the mouth of the same prophet who had spoken the word that smote Bathsheba's first son. In Solomon, God removed Bathsheba's reproach and the reproach of their marriage covenant. God was foreshadowing His love for and restoration of Bathsheba.

Bathsheba is an example to all women who have known pain, immorality, abuse, rejection and slander. She rose above it all and remained true to her faith in, love for and fear of God. Her response to all these injuries could have been very different.

She could have resented David—and God—for the death of her first son. She could have refused to forgive David. Through each hardship she allowed her faith, love and holy fear to guide her response and set her course in life. How different from the royal wife, Michal, who in response to hardship had despised David. God blessed and honored Bathsheba's heart determination. *God caused the wisest king of men to declare her to be the noblest of all women.*

This is an example of the power of the gospel in which we trust. It transforms women with a past into virtuous women with a glorious future. It takes adulteresses and turns them into noble queens. The righteousness of Bathsheba outlived any former maligning of her name.

> Bathsheba rose above it all and remained true to her faith in, love for and fear of God.

Nobility is not merely a function of birth. An individual can be born into the lineage of kings and yet remain a fool. One can be a prince without ever being princely.

Some definitions of the word *noble* are "aristocratic, worthy, virtuous, valorous, gentle, generous, extraordinary, admirable, dignified, remarkable" and more. The word bears the connotation not of birthright but of a righteous life. Nobility is available to king and peasant, rich and poor, male and female. It requires courage and a servant's heart.

Let's delve deeper into the character of this noblewoman, Bathsheba, by drawing on the Amplified Bible and its commentary:

> Many daughters have done...nobly, and well...but you excel them all.
> —PROVERBS 31:29, AMP

This comment exalts Bathsheba above all others who have done noble and well. Her nobility and godliness exceeded all her present peers and her predecessors. She was not a military leader or a public figure; she was a woman at home, a mother, a wife and an instructor in righteousness. Through her godly private life, she rises above—

- *Miriam:* Prophetic praise leader (Exod. 15:20–21)
- *Deborah:* Leader and military adviser (Judg. 4:4–10)
- *Huldah:* Prophetess (2 Kings 22:14)
- *Ruth:* Woman of faithfulness (Ruth 1:16)
- *Hannah:* Ideal wife and mother (1 Sam. 1:20; 2:19)

- *The Shunammite woman:* Gracious hostess (2 Kings 4:8–10)
- *Queen Esther:* Risked her life for her people (Esther 4:16)
- *Abigail:* Intelligent and beautiful (1 Sam. 25:3)
- *Queen of Sheba:* Royal and noble (1 Kings 10)

God elevates His daughters who have developed the fear of the Lord in their lives.

Many of us will never hold such positions of public influence. Yet nobility and valor are available to us in the privacy of our own homes. God elevates His daughters who have developed the fear of the Lord in their lives.

SEVEN VIRTUES

In the Proverbs 31 description, Bathsheba's life exhibits all seven Christian virtues that are later found in 2 Peter 1:5–7:

- Goodness
- Knowledge
- Self-control
- Perseverance
- Godliness
- Brotherly kindness
- Love

Before I drew the parallel that this woman depicted by Solomon was Bathsheba, his mother, I used to read the description of this mysterious and perfect woman and think, *Well, I'd be perfect too if I had her lifestyle—maids and servants to help me, a husband with great influence, my own spending money to buy fields for investment, clothes of fine linen and purple. If I had all this, I'd feel good about myself, and I'd act noble, too!* I dismissed the whole premise of such virtue as unattainable and outdated.

But it wasn't Bathsheba's apparel or lifestyle that made her noble. It was her heart. Nobility is not a function of finances. To prove this point, let's look at another royal beauty. Her response to her beauty and fine provisions was quite different. We find her description in Ezekiel 16:9–14:

> I bathed you with water and washed the blood from you and put ointments on you. I clothed you with an embroidered dress and put leather sandals on you. I dressed you in fine linen and covered you with costly garments. I adorned you with jewelry: I put bracelets on your arms and a necklace around your neck, and I put a ring on your nose, earrings on your ears and a beautiful crown on your head. So you were adorned with gold and silver; your clothes were of fine linen and costly fabric and embroidered cloth. Your food was fine flour, honey and olive oil. You became very beautiful and rose to be a queen. And your fame spread among the nations on account of your beauty, because the splendor I had given you made your beauty perfect, declares the Sovereign LORD.

She was beautiful and dressed in fine linen. She ate the finest food, like the Proverbs 31 woman. She was adorned with the finest jewelry. Like Bathsheba, her beauty alone elevated her to the position of queen. In addition to beauty, God cloaked her in royal splendor and made her beauty perfect.

> But you trusted in your beauty and used your fame to become a prostitute. You lavished your favors on anyone who passed by and your beauty became his.
>
> —EZEKIEL 16:15

Both started out with a cleansing bath. Both were seen naked. Both were later clothed in fine linen. Both were beautiful. Both were queens. Both dined on fine foods. Both had royal children. Both had noble husbands. Both were favored by God. But that is where their similarities ended.

The unfaithful wife trusts in her beauty (Ezek. 16:15), while the noble one trusts in the Lord (Prov. 31:30). Though her nakedness is covered, the faithless wife uncovers her nakedness again (Ezek. 16:36), while the noble wife remains covered and covers the rest of her household in scarlet (Prov. 31:21). The unfaithful wife takes the Lord's provision of food for her and her children and squanders it on idolatry and harlotry (Ezek.

16:20). The faithful wife wisely provides food for her household (Prov. 31:15), then she extends food to the poor and needy (Prov. 31:20).

The faithless woman lives for the moment because she lacks the restraining fear of the Lord.

The faithless wife slaughters and sacrifices her children for her own convenience and advantage (Ezek. 16:21). The noble wife faithfully instructs her children. Her children bless her, while the blood of the wicked woman's children accuses her. The wicked wife squanders the provision of her household in harlotry and riotous promiscuity (Ezek. 16:26, 34). The noble wife watches carefully after her household (Prov. 31:27) and invests wisely. Her husband safely trusts her with everything, knowing she will always do him good (Prov. 31:11–12). There is no trust between the adulteress wife and her husband, only treachery.

The wicked, faithless wife has nothing to look forward to but inevitable and horrible judgment, so she lives for the moment (Ezek. 16:38–41). The noblewoman can laugh with joy at the days ahead of her. There is no fear, worry or dread (Prov. 31:25). She is blessed in this life and eternally rewarded (Prov. 31:29–31).

Women who trust in their own beauty and use the provision of the Lord to seduce and entertain themselves will find that as their beauty fades with age, their former lovers will turn on them. All flesh eventually ages and corrupts. A prostitute's beauty is short-lived and hardens with age. The faithless woman lives for the moment because she lacks the restraining fear of the Lord.

God again describes His rejection of this attitude in Ezekiel 16:49–50:

> Now this was the sin of your sister Sodom: She and her daughters were arrogant, overfed and unconcerned; they did not help the poor and needy. They were haughty and did detestable things before me. Therefore I did away with them as you have seen.

The Sodomites were arrogant, overfed and unconcerned. Their sins were pride, lasciviousness and apathy. They ignored the poor and needy. This self-centered attitude caused them to live a detestable, haughty lifestyle. God did not judge the Sodomites merely for homosexuality; that was just a symptom of a much deeper heart condition. Their proud and wicked hearts led them astray into perversion. God saw the inner motives behind the perverse sexual lifestyle. They were consumed with their luxury and abundance, heaping on themselves and reveling in their own beauty and accomplishments. In this case, inward corruption brought outward destruction.

THE REAL SECRET OF BEAUTY

The noblewoman has learned the secret of a beauty that radiates from within. Her inward purity works an outward radiance. She allows her measure of faith to develop both the love of God and the fear of the Lord in her life.

In order for Bathsheba to train Solomon in the fear of the Lord, she would have first had to realize this fear in her own personal life. I am certain that experiencing the death of a child at God's hand would readily impart a revelation of the fear of God. This holy fear drew her closer to God, not away from Him in cowardice. Though in her time women were not trained in the Scriptures, Bathsheba became educated in the instruction and wisdom of the Lord. She committed herself to raising up a godly son to one day sit on David's throne.

> # The noblewoman has learned the secret of a beauty that radiates from within.

Time and again we hear Bathsheba's wisdom echoed in the words of Solomon. He described her as, "She speaks with wisdom, and faithful instruction is on her tongue" (Prov. 31:26). She imparted a constant practical application in the fear of the Lord for Solomon. She encouraged him to search for it.

My son, if you accept my words and store up my commands within you, turning your ear to wisdom and applying your heart to understanding, and if you call out for insight and cry aloud for understanding, and if you look for it as for silver and search for it as for hidden treasure, then you will understand the fear of the Lord and find the knowledge of God. For the Lord gives wisdom, and from his mouth come knowledge and understanding.

—Proverbs 2:1–6

Wisdom was so ingrained in him that Solomon knew what he wanted before God even asked him. His parents had burned a desire for wisdom and the fear of the Lord into the very fiber of his being. He bore the heartfelt desire of his parents to know God's wisdom and to understand His holy fear. He knew of the brother who had come before him. He'd heard that the Lord loved him and had set him apart as a prince among princes. He knew that only wisdom could preserve and guide his life as king.

WISDOM ABOVE ALL ELSE

Solomon pursued wisdom all his life. As wise as he was, he still strayed by disobeying God's command concerning his foreign wives. They pulled his heart away from following the Lord, and he strayed from following God with his whole heart.

After a prosperous forty-year reign, Solomon looked back on his life and gave this summation of his entire search:

> Now all has been heard; here is the conclusion of the matter: Fear God and keep his commandments, for this is the whole duty of man. For God will bring every deed into judgment, including every hidden thing, whether it is good or evil.
>
> —ECCLESIASTES 12:13–14

At the end of his life, he returns to the wisdom of his parents. He exhorts those who read his words to first fear God and second, to keep His commandments. Why? Because the day will come when each of us must stand before the greatest King and watch as He brings our every word and deed into judgment. Solomon was at the threshold of that judgment and could sense the urgency of what truly merited his time and attention.

As the wisest of all, he knew what was truly valuable. He perceived the scale of God's eternal and true measure. God is the ultimate judge of the true measure of a woman. He is only interested in what remains after the fire of truth purges all the chaff and dross.

Our sexual, sensual, cultural measures of a woman will be consumed before His holiness. Our self-righteous, religious images will crumble under the pressure of His judgment. Our works of the flesh and meaningless activities will appear futile in the light of eternal purpose. How can we endure such judgment?

We cannot. So God covers us.

The Function of the Threefold Cord

The *measure of faith* will cause us to believe that God is just and that He is good. We will embrace the gospel and hide our selves in Christ. This grants us His righteousness. We will place no trust in ourselves or in our own righteousness. Denying ourselves, we will embrace the cross.

The measure of love will draw us closer to God. As we behold Him, we will be transformed by His image into His likeness.

The three strands of faith, love and holy fear—when woven and braided firmly together—provide a safe and sure hold for us.

The fear of God will keep us from returning to the path of destruction. It guards us and cleanses us from impurity. Holy fear imparts a saving knowledge of the Lord. It is the light that draws us nearer, while His love assures us and His faith empowers us.

The three strands of faith, love and holy fear— when woven and braided firmly together—provide a safe and sure hold for us. They are the criteria by which God judges the motivations of our hearts. This standard is not limited merely to women but is applied to all who embrace the cross.

Knowing the fear of the Lord, what manner of women should we be? We must be noble ones, for we are destined for a royal lineage and priesthood. We must strip ourselves of the garments of the world, lay them aside and pick up the pure garments of linen already provided for us.

The faithless woman was washed from her sin and shame only to return and revel in it. God has given each of us a new start, a royal lineage by way of marriage to Him. It no longer matters how we are measured by the world or the Law, for a new and living way has been set before us. Walking in it means leaving behind the old and taking up the new. The old way of measuring ourselves must be buried. You cannot mix the old with the new, for God calls this mixture adultery. One standard of measure has been exchanged for another.

Adapted from *The True Measure of a Woman,* 159–170.

INNER BEAUTY TIP

IF YOU ARE RECEIVING
YOUR AFFIRMATION, LOVE,
SELF-WORTH, JOY, STRENGTH
AND ACCEPTANCE FROM
ANYWHERE BUT GOD,
HE WILL SHAKE IT.

Shake Us
to Wake Us

[The Lord is] like an eagle that stirs up its
nest and hovers over its young, that spreads
its wings to catch them and carries them on
its pinions.

—Deuteronomy 32:11

When God shakes us to wake us, we often find
ourselves surrounded by the unfamiliar and
unfriendly. God wakes us up from the secure by
pushing us out of our comfort zone. By comfort
zone I am referring to all that is familiar, expected,
constant and under our own control.

We are comfortable when what we expect happens. We enjoy being understood and supported
by those around us. We prefer to have a constant
source of financial provision. But when we get all

this comfort and support, we are easily lulled into a false sense of security.

God is more concerned with our condition than our comfort. At times He stirs our nests to make our comforting things uncomfortable.

> [The LORD is] like an eagle that stirs up its nest and hovers over its young, that spreads its wings to catch them and carries them on its pinions.
>
> —DEUTERONOMY 32:11

This is how young eagles get their flight training. They are born into a very comfortable and safe nest, padded and insulated with down from their mother. Meals are flown in fresh daily. But the day comes when their very survival is threatened if they stay in this place of comfort. So the mother eagle makes the welcoming and safe nest uncomfortable and unwelcome.

The mother eagle grabs the nest with her talons and flaps her wings up and down, blowing all the nice, comfortable padding out of the nest. She tears up what she had so carefully provided. Then she takes each baby eagle and carries it outside of the nest into the wind. This is where young eagles learn to fly. You can't try your wings if you're sitting in the nest.

When God's flight training began in earnest in my life, I felt as if there was nothing to hold on to. It seemed my life was a sea of uncertainty. Everything that had been constant was in upheaval or transition. At times it was so intense I would lay in bed, straining my brain trying to figure out why all this upheaval was happening.

God is more concerned with our condition than our comfort.

Our finances were lacking. We were shunned socially. I felt alone, isolated, misunderstood and persecuted. I prayed and cried out to the Lord for direction, only to hear my unanswered questions echoing back at me. I could find no rest.

I felt so conspicuous, as if I were walking around with a huge sign over my head that everyone but me could read. My neediness was so apparent that it repelled people. No one around us seemed to understand why or what we were going through.

I had long since grown weary of trying to explain myself in order to get counsel or some word from the Lord. It seemed no one could help me. There was a reason for that. No one was supposed to. God wanted me to find my answers in Him. He was creating a hunger and restlessness in me.

John was going through the fire, too. At first we would try to discuss it. Maybe we should do this. Perhaps we should never have left Dallas. We are under attack! Soon we found it too confusing to discuss.

John recognized that we were going through a refining process. But I questioned every aspect and detail, trying to make sense of it.

God wanted me to find my answers in Him. He was creating a hunger and restlessness in me.

No Shortcut

One morning John came in excitedly from his time of prayer. God had spoken to him. *At least one person in our house could still hear from God,* I thought excitedly, so I was all ears.

John told me he had been out in a vacant field praying when God instructed him to look around. John noticed a section of short weed grass, then a large plot of dirt followed by an expanse of tall grass.

God told John the short grass represented the anointing he had known on his life; the dirt represented a wilderness he would go through; and the tall grass represented the anointing John would walk in after the wilderness.

I got excited, thinking we were almost through the lonely wilderness time of upheaval. John asked God where he was in the process, wondering if he was near the end of the dirt.

But God was very clear in His answer. "You are at the end of the short grass."

Disappointed, I questioned John, "Is that edifying? Am I supposed to be happy to hear that things are only going to get worse before they get better?"

I wanted a shortcut through the dirt.

Soon I became so busy looking for a way out that I missed the purpose of the process. I was so focused on the desert that I didn't see that the desert was forging the answer to my prayers—that God would create a clean heart in me and that He would separate the precious from the vile.

> Soon I became so busy looking for a way out that I missed the purpose of the process.

One particular evening while feeling exceptionally sorry for myself, I climbed into my bathtub and began to cry. I was six months pregnant with our second son. It appeared quite possible that John could lose his job. I felt persecuted and misunderstood. We believed we were obeying God, so why was all this happening?

John happened to come in and find his large, pregnant wife crying in the tub. He did not even need to ask me what I was crying about. When he looked at me I just poured out every fear, doubt, worry and question I had. "Why, why, why?" I asked.

Calmly John asked me, "Lisa, what have you asked God to do in your life? Did you ask for furniture or clothes?"

At that moment I was silently wishing I had asked for blessings instead of what I was going through.

John probed further, "What did you ask for?"

"I asked God to refine me," I mumbled back.

"Well, that is what you are getting," John answered and walked out.

I knew John was right. It just wasn't what I wanted to hear at the time. I wanted John to say something like, "You poor baby. Here you are pregnant and afraid I'm going to lose my job. Let me comfort you." I did not want him talking to me as if I were a congregation. I wanted sympathy.

"God, even my husband doesn't understand me. Why are You putting me through a transition while I am pregnant?" I complained.

He answered, "Because it is the time when you feel the most vulnerable."

He was definitely right. I felt extremely vulnerable. I was shaky, and He was doing the shaking. God will take the seasons when we feel weak and insecure and use them for our benefit.

> At that time his voice shook the earth, but now he has promised, "Once more I will shake not only the earth but also the heavens. The words "once more" indicate the removing of what can be shaken—that is, created things—so that what cannot be shaken may remain.
>
> —HEBREWS 12:26–27

I was uncomfortable because I was experiencing God's shaking in every aspect of my life. His shaking removes what is temporary and leaves only what is of His kingdom (v. 28). I have since learned to appreciate this process. I want to share five things that shaking accomplishes.

God's shaking removes what is temporary and leaves only what is of His kingdom.

1. It wakes you.

When my children are in a deep sleep, I often have to shake them to rouse them from their slumber. God does the same with His children—waking by shaking. Shaking is definitely not the most pleasant manner in which to be awakened, but it has the most effect. We become wide-awake with our attention captured.

2. It harvests what is ripe.

A few years ago, I lived in Florida where there are plenty of orange groves. When it is citrus harvest time, the citrus growers use machinery with a mechanical arm to grab hold of the trunk of a tree and shake it. The ripe fruit falls into the waiting nets below. Only what is ripe falls freely. God's shaking harvests what is ripe in the life of a believer, both good and bad. We see the product of seeds previously planted.

3. It removes what is dead.

When the wind blows hard enough, it shakes dead leaves from the trees. Dead limbs and branches are also scattered in the wind. Only what is alive stays on the tree and survives the storm.

When God shakes us, only the things of His kingdom will remain. God shakes us to remove our dead works and lifeless limbs. There is no reason to fear the removal of what is old or dead. This paves the way for the new and living. God knows dead works weigh us down and become a fire hazard.

> His work will be shown for what it is, because the Day will bring it to light. It will be revealed with fire, and the fire will test the quality of each man's work.
> —1 CORINTHIANS 3:13

4. IT STRENGTHENS AND ESTABLISHES.

What endures the shaking and remains afterward will be closer to its foundation.

My husband and I once took an international flight that had a layover on the island of Guam, which had just undergone a severe earthquake. All over the island, hotels were in ruins because the builders had not gone to the expense of digging deep enough to find a solid foundation of stone. The buildings shifted during the earthquake and sank until they hit something solid.

Our foundation is to be Jesus Christ. All we labor to build that is not supported by Him will suffer loss.

> For no one can lay any foundation other than the one already laid, which is Jesus Christ...If what he has built survives, he will receive his reward.
> —1 CORINTHIANS 3:11, 14

God shakes so that the things that cannot be shaken will remain. His shaking removes all that is superfluous and that separates or entangles us. This allows us the opportunity to build anew on the proper support structure—Christ.

5. IT UNIFIES.

Imagine putting a cup of red sand and a cup of blue sand into a jar and shaking it. You get purple sand. It would be nearly impossible to separate the red sand from the blue sand again.

When God shakes the church it unites us. We wake up, stop the petty fights and realize what is important.

When we go through a personal shaking, we are knit closer to God. The bonds forged through suffering are harder to break than those made in good times. In the good times we often miss God's presence because we are surrounded by so many others who profess their support and undying loyalty. But when we're suffering, only He remains faithful, strengthening the bond of His love.

> God shakes so that the things that cannot be shaken will remain.

GOD REBUILDS

A note of warning: When God has shaken an area in your life, don't try to rebuild it yourself. Allow Him to restore only those things He wants to establish in your life. Remember, He is the one doing the shaking.

He is shaking our homes to find out what they are grounded on. This shaking will expose any hidden idols in our lives. An idol is what we give our strength to or draw our strength from.

If you are receiving your affirmation, love, self-worth, joy, strength and acceptance from anywhere but God, He will shake it. He does not do this to upset you; He does it so you will get your life from Him. He knows everything else will eventually disappoint you.

After a shaking we see our condition in relation to God's truth. We see ourselves in comparison to God's standard.

When we submit to God's truth we experience freedom. Liberty remains if we become responsible and accountable. It is not the truth you know but the truth you live that sets you free. To be responsible we must be obedient.

> # When we submit to God's truth we experience freedom.

We would not grant as much liberty to a disobedient or rebellious child as we would grant to an obedient and responsible child. A disobedient child would use his liberty to rebel. He would confuse rebellion for freedom. Rebellion does not foster liberty; it brings bondage. Only through obedience can we find true liberty. As the Holy Spirit ministers truth to your heart, receive it and walk in it. Let God's Word be made flesh in your life.

Adapted from *Out of Control and Loving It!*, 63–70.

Conclusion

Have you ever seen a calf released from its stall? As soon as the door is opened it bolts, leaping, kicking, bounding and stretching. Watching this, you begin to wonder how the stall ever contained it!

> But for you who revere my name, the sun of righteousness will rise with healing in its wings. And you will go out and leap like calves released from the stall.
> —MALACHI 4:2

God used this analogy to describe the release of His own people, those who revere and honor His name. They had been pinned up in a stall. Now He wants them free to feed and frolic in the fields.

Notice that before He frees them He is going to heal them. His sun of righteousness will arise with healing. The sun is a ball of constant and consuming

79

fire. We can be certain God is speaking about fire, for in Malachi 4:1 it says:

> "Surely the day is coming; it will burn like a furnace. All the arrogant and every evildoer will be stubble, and that day that is coming will set them on fire," says the LORD Almighty. "Not a root or a branch will be left to them."

This describes the refining fire of God's judgment on the proud and wicked. It will burn them until there is nothing left. The same fire that destroys them will purify and heal the believers who love and fear God. The Word of God gives light and life to us, but the same Word pronounces judgment on the world of unbelievers.

After God heals and releases us, we will "trample down the wicked; they will be ashes under the soles of your feet on the day when I do these things" (Mal. 4:3). Are you ready to be released? Are you ready to begin living with an understanding of the true measure of a woman of God? Do you want to radiate the inner beauty God has placed in you as a reflection of His very own glory?

Something higher awaits you, a freedom like none you've ever known.

Something higher awaits you, a freedom like none you've ever known. It is a priceless freedom that you must fight to maintain. Yet you must allow God to be the One to judge those around you. You need only to submit to God's refining and healing process.

I believe the truths in this book are part of that process. You will know the truth, and it will set you free. It will release you from all captivity.

Adapted from *Out of Control and Loving It!*, 173–174.

Don't read just one! This book is part of a series.

Check out the rest of the *Inner Beauty Series* by Lisa Bevere.

All books are just $8.99 each

Understand Your True Measure
Come face to face with who you are in Christ and learn how to work through your personal discoveries.

Put Away Your Past
Don't let the enemy rub your nose in your less-than-perfect past! Regardless of the past, God has a plan for you.

Look Beyond What You See
God sees you differently than you see yourself. Let God define and refine you!

Discover Your Inner Beauty
Discover your true righteousness in Christ, which radiates beauty from the inside out.

Give Up and Get Free
Stop trying so hard—allow God to take control! Experience what true freedom really is!

TO ORDER, CALL 1-800-599-5750

or visit your local Christian bookstore or
www.charismahouse.com

If you are enjoying the Inner Beauty Series by Lisa Bevere, here are some other titles from Charisma House that we think will minister to you…

Out of Control and Loving It!
Lisa Bevere
ISBN: 0-88419-436-1
Retail Price: $12.99

Lisa Bevere's life was a whirlwind of turmoil until she discovered that whenever she was in charge, things ended up in a mess. *Out of Control and Loving It!* is her journey from fearful, frantic control to a haven of rest and peace under God's control.

You Are Not What You Weigh
Lisa Bevere
ISBN: 0-88419-661-5
Retail Price: $10.99

Are you tired of reading trendy diet books, taking faddish pills and ordering the latest in infomercial exercise equipment? This is not another "how-to-lose-weight" book. Dare to believe, and this will be the last book you'll need to finally end your war with food and break free from the bondage of weight watching.

The True Measure of a Woman
Lisa Bevere
ISBN: 0-88419-487-6
Retail Price: $11.99

In her frank, yet gentle manner, Lisa Bevere exposes the subtle influences and blatant lies that hold many women captive. With the unveiling truth of God's Word, she displaces these lies and helps you discover who you are in Christ.

 To pick up a copy of any of these titles, contact your local Christian bookstore or order online at www.charismawarehouse.com.